The pages in this notepad should help you analyze decisions in your life, both big and small. The important part of any pro and con list is to make sure you weigh all of the pros and cons, and then come to a conclusion based on the numbers, not just the number of pros and cons.

Another helpful thing is to know that the lists you generate are from your perspective. If you want to make a decision that affects other people, it might be useful to rip out a page and hand it over to them to fill out. Or, you can work together on a list and then get their weight (from 1 to 5) on each item. You may find their responses vastly different from yours, and that's the point. You can then average everything together and come to a total.

Once you have the data, your next step should be to act on the decision. There is no point in making the list just for the sake of making the list. Think, decide, and act.

Note: There are pages near the end of this notepad to reserved for decisions that need a little more space for pros and cons.

Date:

Write down the decision you want to analyze.

_____

_____

Write down the pros (positives) and cons (negatives) related to the above. Give each one a number, 1-5 where 1 is not very important and 5 is extremely important. You don't need to fill out all the spaces.

PROS	1-5	CONS	1-5
TOTAL		TOTAL	

Add up the totals. What is your conclusion and what are your next steps?

_____

_____

Date:

Write down the decision you want to analyze.

_____

_____

Write down the pros (positives) and cons (negatives) related to the above. Give each one a number, 1-5 where 1 is not very important and 5 is extremely important. You don't need to fill out all the spaces.

PROS	1-5	CONS	1-5
TOTAL		TOTAL	

Add up the totals. What is your conclusion and what are your next steps?

_____

_____

Date:

Write down the decision you want to analyze.

_____

_____

Write down the pros (positives) and cons (negatives) related to the above. Give each one a number, 1-5 where 1 is not very important and 5 is extremely important. You don't need to fill out all the spaces.

PROS	1-5	CONS	1-5
TOTAL		TOTAL	

Add up the totals. What is your conclusion and what are your next steps?

_____

_____

Date:

Write down the decision you want to analyze.

_____

_____

Write down the pros (positives) and cons (negatives) related to the above. Give
each one a number, 1-5 where 1 is not very important and 5 is extremely
important. You don't need to fill out all the spaces.

PROS	1-5	CONS	1-5
TOTAL		TOTAL	

Add up the totals. What is your conclusion and what are your next steps?

_____

_____

Date:

Write down the decision you want to analyze.

_____

_____

Write down the pros (positives) and cons (negatives) related to the above. Give each one a number, 1-5 where 1 is not very important and 5 is extremely important. You don't need to fill out all the spaces.

PROS	1-5	CONS	1-5
TOTAL		TOTAL	

Add up the totals. What is your conclusion and what are your next steps?

_____

_____

Date:

Write down the decision you want to analyze.

_____

_____

Write down the pros (positives) and cons (negatives) related to the above. Give each one a number, 1-5 where 1 is not very important and 5 is extremely important. You don't need to fill out all the spaces.

PROS	1-5	CONS	1-5
TOTAL		TOTAL	

Add up the totals. What is your conclusion and what are your next steps?

_____

_____

Date:

Write down the decision you want to analyze.

_____

_____

Write down the pros (positives) and cons (negatives) related to the above. Give each one a number, 1-5 where 1 is not very important and 5 is extremely important. You don't need to fill out all the spaces.

PROS	1-5	CONS	1-5
TOTAL		TOTAL	

Add up the totals. What is your conclusion and what are your next steps?

_____

_____

Date:

Write down the decision you want to analyze.

_____

_____

Write down the pros (positives) and cons (negatives) related to the above. Give
each one a number, 1-5 where 1 is not very important and 5 is extremely
important. You don't need to fill out all the spaces.

PROS	1-5	CONS	1-5
TOTAL		TOTAL	

Add up the totals. What is your conclusion and what are your next steps?

_____

_____

Date:

Write down the decision you want to analyze.

_____

_____

Write down the pros (positives) and cons (negatives) related to the above. Give each one a number, 1-5 where 1 is not very important and 5 is extremely important. You don't need to fill out all the spaces.

PROS	1-5	CONS	1-5
TOTAL		TOTAL	

Add up the totals. What is your conclusion and what are your next steps?

_____

_____

Date:

Write down the decision you want to analyze.

_____

_____

Write down the pros (positives) and cons (negatives) related to the above. Give each one a number, 1-5 where 1 is not very important and 5 is extremely important. You don't need to fill out all the spaces.

PROS	1-5	CONS	1-5
TOTAL		TOTAL	

Add up the totals. What is your conclusion and what are your next steps?

_____

_____

Date:

Write down the decision you want to analyze.

_____

_____

Write down the pros (positives) and cons (negatives) related to the above. Give each one a number, 1-5 where 1 is not very important and 5 is extremely important. You don't need to fill out all the spaces.

PROS	1-5	CONS	1-5
TOTAL		TOTAL	

Add up the totals. What is your conclusion and what are your next steps?

_____

_____

Date:

Write down the decision you want to analyze.

_____

_____

Write down the pros (positives) and cons (negatives) related to the above. Give each one a number, 1-5 where 1 is not very important and 5 is extremely important. You don't need to fill out all the spaces.

PROS	1-5	CONS	1-5
TOTAL		TOTAL	

Add up the totals. What is your conclusion and what are your next steps?

_____

_____

Date:

Write down the decision you want to analyze.

_____

_____

Write down the pros (positives) and cons (negatives) related to the above. Give each one a number, 1-5 where 1 is not very important and 5 is extremely important. You don't need to fill out all the spaces.

PROS	1-5	CONS	1-5
TOTAL		TOTAL	

Add up the totals. What is your conclusion and what are your next steps?

_____

_____

Date:

Write down the decision you want to analyze.

_____

_____

Write down the pros (positives) and cons (negatives) related to the above. Give each one a number, 1-5 where 1 is not very important and 5 is extremely important. You don't need to fill out all the spaces.

PROS	1-5	CONS	1-5
TOTAL		TOTAL	

Add up the totals. What is your conclusion and what are your next steps?

_____

_____

Date:

Write down the decision you want to analyze.

_____

_____

Write down the pros (positives) and cons (negatives) related to the above. Give each one a number, 1-5 where 1 is not very important and 5 is extremely important. You don't need to fill out all the spaces.

PROS	1-5	CONS	1-5
TOTAL		TOTAL	

Add up the totals. What is your conclusion and what are your next steps?

_____

_____

Date:

Write down the decision you want to analyze.

_____

_____

Write down the pros (positives) and cons (negatives) related to the above. Give
each one a number, 1-5 where 1 is not very important and 5 is extremely
important. You don't need to fill out all the spaces.

PROS	1-5	CONS	1-5
TOTAL		TOTAL	

Add up the totals. What is your conclusion and what are your next steps?

_____

_____

Date:

Write down the decision you want to analyze.

_____

_____

Write down the pros (positives) and cons (negatives) related to the above. Give each one a number, 1-5 where 1 is not very important and 5 is extremely important. You don't need to fill out all the spaces.

PROS	1-5	CONS	1-5
TOTAL		TOTAL	

Add up the totals. What is your conclusion and what are your next steps?

_____

_____

Date:

Write down the decision you want to analyze.

_____

_____

Write down the pros (positives) and cons (negatives) related to the above. Give
each one a number, 1-5 where 1 is not very important and 5 is extremely
important. You don't need to fill out all the spaces.

PROS	1-5	CONS	1-5
TOTAL		TOTAL	

Add up the totals. What is your conclusion and what are your next steps?

_____

_____

Date:

Write down the decision you want to analyze.

_____

_____

Write down the pros (positives) and cons (negatives) related to the above. Give each one a number, 1-5 where 1 is not very important and 5 is extremely important. You don't need to fill out all the spaces.

PROS	1-5	CONS	1-5
TOTAL		TOTAL	

Add up the totals. What is your conclusion and what are your next steps?

_____

_____

Date:

Write down the decision you want to analyze.

_____

_____

Write down the pros (positives) and cons (negatives) related to the above. Give each one a number, 1-5 where 1 is not very important and 5 is extremely important. You don't need to fill out all the spaces.

PROS	1-5	CONS	1-5
TOTAL		TOTAL	

Add up the totals. What is your conclusion and what are your next steps?

_____

_____

Date:

Write down the decision you want to analyze.

_____

_____

Write down the pros (positives) and cons (negatives) related to the above. Give each one a number, 1-5 where 1 is not very important and 5 is extremely important. You don't need to fill out all the spaces.

PROS	1-5	CONS	1-5
TOTAL		TOTAL	

Add up the totals. What is your conclusion and what are your next steps?

_____

_____

Date:

Write down the decision you want to analyze.

_____

_____

Write down the pros (positives) and cons (negatives) related to the above. Give each one a number, 1-5 where 1 is not very important and 5 is extremely important. You don't need to fill out all the spaces.

PROS	1-5	CONS	1-5
TOTAL		TOTAL	

Add up the totals. What is your conclusion and what are your next steps?

_____

_____

Date:

Write down the decision you want to analyze.

_____

_____

Write down the pros (positives) and cons (negatives) related to the above. Give
each one a number, 1-5 where 1 is not very important and 5 is extremely
important. You don't need to fill out all the spaces.

PROS	1-5	CONS	1-5
TOTAL		TOTAL	

Add up the totals. What is your conclusion and what are your next steps?

_____

_____

Date:

Write down the decision you want to analyze.

_____

_____

Write down the pros (positives) and cons (negatives) related to the above. Give each one a number, 1-5 where 1 is not very important and 5 is extremely important. You don't need to fill out all the spaces.

PROS	1-5	CONS	1-5
TOTAL		TOTAL	

Add up the totals. What is your conclusion and what are your next steps?

_____

_____

Date:

Write down the decision you want to analyze.

_____

_____

Write down the pros (positives) and cons (negatives) related to the above. Give each one a number, 1-5 where 1 is not very important and 5 is extremely important. You don't need to fill out all the spaces.

PROS	1-5	CONS	1-5
TOTAL		TOTAL	

Add up the totals. What is your conclusion and what are your next steps?

_____

_____

Date:

Write down the decision you want to analyze.

_____

_____

Write down the pros (positives) and cons (negatives) related to the above. Give each one a number, 1-5 where 1 is not very important and 5 is extremely important. You don't need to fill out all the spaces.

PROS	1-5	CONS	1-5
TOTAL		TOTAL	

Add up the totals. What is your conclusion and what are your next steps?

_____

_____

Date:

Write down the decision you want to analyze.

_____

_____

Write down the pros (positives) and cons (negatives) related to the above. Give each one a number, 1-5 where 1 is not very important and 5 is extremely important. You don't need to fill out all the spaces.

PROS	1-5	CONS	1-5
TOTAL		TOTAL	

Add up the totals. What is your conclusion and what are your next steps?

_____

_____

Date:

Write down the decision you want to analyze.

_____

_____

Write down the pros (positives) and cons (negatives) related to the above. Give each one a number, 1-5 where 1 is not very important and 5 is extremely important. You don't need to fill out all the spaces.

PROS	1-5	CONS	1-5
TOTAL		TOTAL	

Add up the totals. What is your conclusion and what are your next steps?

_____

_____

Date:

Write down the decision you want to analyze.

_____

_____

Write down the pros (positives) and cons (negatives) related to the above. Give each one a number, 1-5 where 1 is not very important and 5 is extremely important. You don't need to fill out all the spaces.

PROS	1-5	CONS	1-5
TOTAL		TOTAL	

Add up the totals. What is your conclusion and what are your next steps?

_____

_____

Date:

Write down the decision you want to analyze.

_____

_____

Write down the pros (positives) and cons (negatives) related to the above. Give
each one a number, 1-5 where 1 is not very important and 5 is extremely
important. You don't need to fill out all the spaces.

PROS	1-5	CONS	1-5
TOTAL		TOTAL	

Add up the totals. What is your conclusion and what are your next steps?

_____

_____

Date:

Write down the decision you want to analyze.

_____

_____

Write down the pros (positives) and cons (negatives) related to the above. Give each one a number, 1-5 where 1 is not very important and 5 is extremely important. You don't need to fill out all the spaces.

PROS	1-5	CONS	1-5
TOTAL		TOTAL	

Add up the totals. What is your conclusion and what are your next steps?

_____

_____

Date:

Write down the decision you want to analyze.

_____

_____

Write down the pros (positives) and cons (negatives) related to the above. Give
each one a number, 1-5 where 1 is not very important and 5 is extremely
important. You don't need to fill out all the spaces.

PROS	1-5	CONS	1-5
TOTAL		TOTAL	

Add up the totals. What is your conclusion and what are your next steps?

_____

_____

Date:

Write down the decision you want to analyze.

_____

_____

Write down the pros (positives) and cons (negatives) related to the above. Give each one a number, 1-5 where 1 is not very important and 5 is extremely important. You don't need to fill out all the spaces.

PROS	1-5	CONS	1-5
TOTAL		TOTAL	

Add up the totals. What is your conclusion and what are your next steps?

_____

_____

Date:

Write down the decision you want to analyze.

_____

_____

Write down the pros (positives) and cons (negatives) related to the above. Give each one a number, 1-5 where 1 is not very important and 5 is extremely important. You don't need to fill out all the spaces.

PROS	1-5	CONS	1-5
TOTAL		TOTAL	

Add up the totals. What is your conclusion and what are your next steps?

_____

_____

Date:

Write down the decision you want to analyze.

_____

_____

Write down the pros (positives) and cons (negatives) related to the above. Give each one a number, 1-5 where 1 is not very important and 5 is extremely important. You don't need to fill out all the spaces.

PROS	1-5	CONS	1-5
TOTAL		TOTAL	

Add up the totals. What is your conclusion and what are your next steps?

_____

_____

Date:

Write down the decision you want to analyze.

_____

_____

Write down the pros (positives) and cons (negatives) related to the above. Give each one a number, 1-5 where 1 is not very important and 5 is extremely important. You don't need to fill out all the spaces.

PROS	1-5	CONS	1-5
TOTAL		TOTAL	

Add up the totals. What is your conclusion and what are your next steps?

_____

_____

Date:

Write down the decision you want to analyze.

_____

_____

Write down the pros (positives) and cons (negatives) related to the above. Give each one a number, 1-5 where 1 is not very important and 5 is extremely important. You don't need to fill out all the spaces.

PROS	1-5	CONS	1-5
TOTAL		TOTAL	

Add up the totals. What is your conclusion and what are your next steps?

_____

_____

Date:

Write down the decision you want to analyze.

_____

_____

Write down the pros (positives) and cons (negatives) related to the above. Give each one a number, 1-5 where 1 is not very important and 5 is extremely important. You don't need to fill out all the spaces.

PROS	1-5	CONS	1-5
TOTAL		TOTAL	

Add up the totals. What is your conclusion and what are your next steps?

_____

_____

Date:

Write down the decision you want to analyze.

_____

_____

Write down the pros (positives) and cons (negatives) related to the above. Give each one a number, 1-5 where 1 is not very important and 5 is extremely important. You don't need to fill out all the spaces.

PROS	1-5	CONS	1-5
TOTAL		TOTAL	

Add up the totals. What is your conclusion and what are your next steps?

_____

_____

Date:

Write down the decision you want to analyze.

_____

_____

Write down the pros (positives) and cons (negatives) related to the above. Give each one a number, 1-5 where 1 is not very important and 5 is extremely important. You don't need to fill out all the spaces.

PROS	1-5	CONS	1-5
TOTAL		TOTAL	

Add up the totals. What is your conclusion and what are your next steps?

_____

_____

Date:

Write down the decision you want to analyze.

_____

_____

Write down the pros (positives) and cons (negatives) related to the above. Give each one a number, 1-5 where 1 is not very important and 5 is extremely important. You don't need to fill out all the spaces.

PROS	1-5	CONS	1-5
TOTAL		TOTAL	

Add up the totals. What is your conclusion and what are your next steps?

_____

_____

Date:

Write down the decision you want to analyze.

_____

_____

Write down the pros (positives) and cons (negatives) related to the above. Give each one a number, 1-5 where 1 is not very important and 5 is extremely important. You don't need to fill out all the spaces.

PROS	1-5	CONS	1-5
TOTAL		TOTAL	

Add up the totals. What is your conclusion and what are your next steps?

_____

_____

Date:

Write down the decision you want to analyze.

_____

_____

Write down the pros (positives) and cons (negatives) related to the above. Give each one a number, 1-5 where 1 is not very important and 5 is extremely important. You don't need to fill out all the spaces.

PROS	1-5	CONS	1-5
TOTAL		TOTAL	

Add up the totals. What is your conclusion and what are your next steps?

_____

_____

Date:

Write down the decision you want to analyze.

_____

_____

Write down the pros (positives) and cons (negatives) related to the above. Give each one a number, 1-5 where 1 is not very important and 5 is extremely important. You don't need to fill out all the spaces.

PROS	1-5	CONS	1-5
TOTAL		TOTAL	

Add up the totals. What is your conclusion and what are your next steps?

_____

_____

Date:

Write down the decision you want to analyze.

_____

_____

Write down the pros (positives) and cons (negatives) related to the above. Give each one a number, 1-5 where 1 is not very important and 5 is extremely important. You don't need to fill out all the spaces.

PROS	1-5	CONS	1-5
TOTAL		TOTAL	

Add up the totals. What is your conclusion and what are your next steps?

_____

_____

Date:

Write down the decision you want to analyze.

_____

_____

Write down the pros (positives) and cons (negatives) related to the above. Give each one a number, 1-5 where 1 is not very important and 5 is extremely important. You don't need to fill out all the spaces.

PROS	1-5	CONS	1-5
TOTAL		TOTAL	

Add up the totals. What is your conclusion and what are your next steps?

_____

_____

Date:

Write down the decision you want to analyze.

_____

_____

Write down the pros (positives) and cons (negatives) related to the above. Give each one a number, 1-5 where 1 is not very important and 5 is extremely important. You don't need to fill out all the spaces.

PROS	1-5	CONS	1-5
TOTAL		TOTAL	

Add up the totals. What is your conclusion and what are your next steps?

_____

_____

Date:

Write down the decision you want to analyze.

_____

_____

Write down the pros (positives) and cons (negatives) related to the above. Give each one a number, 1-5 where 1 is not very important and 5 is extremely important. You don't need to fill out all the spaces.

PROS	1-5	CONS	1-5
TOTAL		TOTAL	

Add up the totals. What is your conclusion and what are your next steps?

_____

_____

Date:

Write down the decision you want to analyze.

_____

_____

Write down the pros (positives) and cons (negatives) related to the above. Give each one a number, 1-5 where 1 is not very important and 5 is extremely important. You don't need to fill out all the spaces.

PROS	1-5	CONS	1-5
TOTAL		TOTAL	

Add up the totals. What is your conclusion and what are your next steps?

_____

_____

Date:

Write down the decision you want to analyze.

_____

_____

Write down the pros (positives) and cons (negatives) related to the above. Give each one a number, 1-5 where 1 is not very important and 5 is extremely important. You don't need to fill out all the spaces.

PROS	1-5	CONS	1-5
TOTAL		TOTAL	

Add up the totals. What is your conclusion and what are your next steps?

_____

_____

Date:

Write down the decision you want to analyze.

_____

_____

Write down the pros (positives) and cons (negatives) related to the above. Give each one a number, 1-5 where 1 is not very important and 5 is extremely important. You don't need to fill out all the spaces.

PROS	1-5	CONS	1-5
TOTAL		TOTAL	

Add up the totals. What is your conclusion and what are your next steps?

_____

_____

Date:

Write down the decision you want to analyze.

_____

_____

Write down the pros (positives) and cons (negatives) related to the above. Give each one a number, 1-5 where 1 is not very important and 5 is extremely important. You don't need to fill out all the spaces.

PROS	1-5	CONS	1-5
TOTAL		TOTAL	

Add up the totals. What is your conclusion and what are your next steps?

_____

_____

Date:

Write down the decision you want to analyze.

_____

_____

Write down the pros (positives) and cons (negatives) related to the above. Give each one a number, 1-5 where 1 is not very important and 5 is extremely important. You don't need to fill out all the spaces.

PROS	1-5	CONS	1-5
TOTAL		TOTAL	

Add up the totals. What is your conclusion and what are your next steps?

_____

_____

Date:

Write down the decision you want to analyze.

_____

_____

Write down the pros (positives) and cons (negatives) related to the above. Give each one a number, 1-5 where 1 is not very important and 5 is extremely important. You don't need to fill out all the spaces.

PROS	1-5	CONS	1-5
TOTAL		TOTAL	

Add up the totals. What is your conclusion and what are your next steps?

_____

_____

Date:

Write down the decision you want to analyze.

_____

_____

Write down the pros (positives) and cons (negatives) related to the above. Give each one a number, 1-5 where 1 is not very important and 5 is extremely important. You don't need to fill out all the spaces.

PROS	1-5	CONS	1-5
TOTAL		TOTAL	

Add up the totals. What is your conclusion and what are your next steps?

_____

_____

Date:

Write down the decision you want to analyze.

_____

_____

Write down the pros (positives) and cons (negatives) related to the above. Give each one a number, 1-5 where 1 is not very important and 5 is extremely important. You don't need to fill out all the spaces.

PROS	1-5	CONS	1-5
TOTAL		TOTAL	

Add up the totals. What is your conclusion and what are your next steps?

_____

_____

Date:

Write down the decision you want to analyze.

_____

_____

Write down the pros (positives) and cons (negatives) related to the above. Give each one a number, 1-5 where 1 is not very important and 5 is extremely important. You don't need to fill out all the spaces.

PROS	1-5	CONS	1-5
TOTAL		TOTAL	

Add up the totals. What is your conclusion and what are your next steps?

_____

_____

Date:

Write down the decision you want to analyze.

_____

_____

Write down the pros (positives) and cons (negatives) related to the above. Give each one a number, 1-5 where 1 is not very important and 5 is extremely important. You don't need to fill out all the spaces.

PROS	1-5	CONS	1-5
TOTAL		TOTAL	

Add up the totals. What is your conclusion and what are your next steps?

_____

_____

Date:

Write down the decision you want to analyze.

_____

_____

Write down the pros (positives) and cons (negatives) related to the above. Give each one a number, 1-5 where 1 is not very important and 5 is extremely important. You don't need to fill out all the spaces.

PROS	1-5	CONS	1-5
TOTAL		TOTAL	

Add up the totals. What is your conclusion and what are your next steps?

_____

_____

Date:

Write down the decision you want to analyze.

_____

_____

Write down the pros (positives) and cons (negatives) related to the above. Give each one a number, 1-5 where 1 is not very important and 5 is extremely important. You don't need to fill out all the spaces.

PROS	1-5	CONS	1-5
TOTAL		TOTAL	

Add up the totals. What is your conclusion and what are your next steps?

_____

_____

Date:

Write down the decision you want to analyze.

_____

_____

Write down the pros (positives) and cons (negatives) related to the above. Give each one a number, 1-5 where 1 is not very important and 5 is extremely important. You don't need to fill out all the spaces.

PROS	1-5	CONS	1-5
TOTAL		TOTAL	

Add up the totals. What is your conclusion and what are your next steps?

_____

_____

Date:

Write down the decision you want to analyze.

_____

_____

Write down the pros (positives) and cons (negatives) related to the above. Give each one a number, 1-5 where 1 is not very important and 5 is extremely important. You don't need to fill out all the spaces.

PROS	1-5	CONS	1-5
TOTAL		TOTAL	

Add up the totals. What is your conclusion and what are your next steps?

_____

_____

Date:

Write down the decision you want to analyze.

_____

_____

Write down the pros (positives) and cons (negatives) related to the above. Give each one a number, 1-5 where 1 is not very important and 5 is extremely important. You don't need to fill out all the spaces.

PROS	1-5	CONS	1-5
TOTAL		TOTAL	

Add up the totals. What is your conclusion and what are your next steps?

_____

_____

Date:

Write down the decision you want to analyze.

_____

_____

Write down the pros (positives) and cons (negatives) related to the above. Give each one a number, 1-5 where 1 is not very important and 5 is extremely important. You don't need to fill out all the spaces.

PROS	1-5	CONS	1-5
TOTAL		TOTAL	

Add up the totals. What is your conclusion and what are your next steps?

_____

_____

Date:

Write down the decision you want to analyze.

_____

_____

Write down the pros (positives) and cons (negatives) related to the above. Give each one a number, 1-5 where 1 is not very important and 5 is extremely important. You don't need to fill out all the spaces.

PROS	1-5	CONS	1-5
TOTAL		TOTAL	

Add up the totals. What is your conclusion and what are your next steps?

_____

_____

Date:

Write down the decision you want to analyze.

_____

_____

Write down the pros (positives) and cons (negatives) related to the above. Give each one a number, 1-5 where 1 is not very important and 5 is extremely important. You don't need to fill out all the spaces.

PROS	1-5	CONS	1-5
TOTAL		TOTAL	

Add up the totals. What is your conclusion and what are your next steps?

_____

_____

Date:

Write down the decision you want to analyze.

_____

_____

Write down the pros (positives) and cons (negatives) related to the above. Give each one a number, 1-5 where 1 is not very important and 5 is extremely important. You don't need to fill out all the spaces.

PROS	1-5	CONS	1-5
TOTAL		TOTAL	

Add up the totals. What is your conclusion and what are your next steps?

_____

_____

Date:

Write down the decision you want to analyze.

_____

_____

Write down the pros (positives) and cons (negatives) related to the above. Give each one a number, 1-5 where 1 is not very important and 5 is extremely important. You don't need to fill out all the spaces.

PROS	1-5	CONS	1-5
TOTAL		TOTAL	

Add up the totals. What is your conclusion and what are your next steps?

_____

_____

Date:

Write down the decision you want to analyze.

_____

_____

Write down the pros (positives) and cons (negatives) related to the above. Give each one a number, 1-5 where 1 is not very important and 5 is extremely important. You don't need to fill out all the spaces.

PROS	1-5	CONS	1-5
TOTAL		TOTAL	

Add up the totals. What is your conclusion and what are your next steps?

_____

_____

Date:

Write down the decision you want to analyze.

_____

_____

Write down the pros (positives) and cons (negatives) related to the above. Give each one a number, 1-5 where 1 is not very important and 5 is extremely important. You don't need to fill out all the spaces.

PROS	1-5	CONS	1-5
TOTAL		TOTAL	

Add up the totals. What is your conclusion and what are your next steps?

_____

_____

Date:

Write down the decision you want to analyze.

_____

_____

Write down the pros (positives) and cons (negatives) related to the above. Give each one a number, 1-5 where 1 is not very important and 5 is extremely important. You don't need to fill out all the spaces.

PROS	1-5	CONS	1-5
TOTAL		TOTAL	

Add up the totals. What is your conclusion and what are your next steps?

_____

_____

Date:

Write down the decision you want to analyze.

_____

_____

Write down the pros (positives) and cons (negatives) related to the above. Give each one a number, 1-5 where 1 is not very important and 5 is extremely important. You don't need to fill out all the spaces.

PROS	1-5	CONS	1-5
TOTAL		TOTAL	

Add up the totals. What is your conclusion and what are your next steps?

_____

_____

Date:

Write down the decision you want to analyze.

_____

_____

Write down the pros (positives) and cons (negatives) related to the above. Give each one a number, 1-5 where 1 is not very important and 5 is extremely important. You don't need to fill out all the spaces.

PROS	1-5	CONS	1-5
TOTAL		TOTAL	

Add up the totals. What is your conclusion and what are your next steps?

_____

_____

Date:

Write down the decision you want to analyze.

_____

_____

Write down the pros (positives) and cons (negatives) related to the above. Give each one a number, 1-5 where 1 is not very important and 5 is extremely important. You don't need to fill out all the spaces.

PROS	1-5	CONS	1-5
TOTAL		TOTAL	

Add up the totals. What is your conclusion and what are your next steps?

_____

_____

Date:

Write down the decision you want to analyze.

_____

_____

Write down the pros (positives) and cons (negatives) related to the above. Give each one a number, 1-5 where 1 is not very important and 5 is extremely important. You don't need to fill out all the spaces.

PROS	1-5	CONS	1-5
TOTAL		TOTAL	

Add up the totals. What is your conclusion and what are your next steps?

_____

_____

Date:

Write down the decision you want to analyze.

_____

_____

Write down the pros (positives) and cons (negatives) related to the above. Give each one a number, 1-5 where 1 is not very important and 5 is extremely important. You don't need to fill out all the spaces.

PROS	1-5	CONS	1-5
TOTAL		TOTAL	

Add up the totals. What is your conclusion and what are your next steps?

_____

_____

Date:

Write down the decision you want to analyze.

_____

_____

Write down the pros (positives) and cons (negatives) related to the above. Give each one a number, 1-5 where 1 is not very important and 5 is extremely important. You don't need to fill out all the spaces.

PROS	1-5	CONS	1-5
TOTAL		TOTAL	

Add up the totals. What is your conclusion and what are your next steps?

_____

_____

Date:

Write down the decision you want to analyze.

_____

_____

Write down the pros (positives) and cons (negatives) related to the above. Give each one a number, 1-5 where 1 is not very important and 5 is extremely important. You don't need to fill out all the spaces.

PROS	1-5	CONS	1-5
TOTAL		TOTAL	

Add up the totals. What is your conclusion and what are your next steps?

_____

_____

Date:

Write down the decision you want to analyze.

_____

_____

Write down the pros (positives) and cons (negatives) related to the above. Give each one a number, 1-5 where 1 is not very important and 5 is extremely important. You don't need to fill out all the spaces.

PROS	1-5	CONS	1-5
TOTAL		TOTAL	

Add up the totals. What is your conclusion and what are your next steps?

_____

_____

Date:

Write down the decision you want to analyze.

_____

_____

Write down the pros (positives) and cons (negatives) related to the above. Give each one a number, 1-5 where 1 is not very important and 5 is extremely important. You don't need to fill out all the spaces.

PROS	1-5	CONS	1-5
TOTAL		TOTAL	

Add up the totals. What is your conclusion and what are your next steps?

_____

_____

Date:

Write down the decision you want to analyze.

_____

_____

Write down the pros (positives) and cons (negatives) related to the above. Give each one a number, 1-5 where 1 is not very important and 5 is extremely important. You don't need to fill out all the spaces.

PROS	1-5	CONS	1-5
TOTAL		TOTAL	

Add up the totals. What is your conclusion and what are your next steps?

_____

_____

Date:

Write down the decision you want to analyze.

_____

_____

Write down the pros (positives) and cons (negatives) related to the above. Give each one a number, 1-5 where 1 is not very important and 5 is extremely important. You don't need to fill out all the spaces.

PROS	1-5	CONS	1-5
TOTAL		TOTAL	

Add up the totals. What is your conclusion and what are your next steps?

_____

_____

Date:

Write down the decision you want to analyze.

_____

_____

Write down the pros (positives) and cons (negatives) related to the above. Give each one a number, 1-5 where 1 is not very important and 5 is extremely important. You don't need to fill out all the spaces.

PROS	1-5	CONS	1-5
TOTAL		TOTAL	

Add up the totals. What is your conclusion and what are your next steps?

_____

_____

Date:

Write down the decision you want to analyze.

_____

_____

Write down the pros (positives) and cons (negatives) related to the above. Give each one a number, 1-5 where 1 is not very important and 5 is extremely important. You don't need to fill out all the spaces.

PROS	1-5	CONS	1-5
TOTAL		TOTAL	

Add up the totals. What is your conclusion and what are your next steps?

_____

_____

Date:

Write down the decision you want to analyze.

_____

_____

Write down the pros (positives) and cons (negatives) related to the above. Give each one a number, 1-5 where 1 is not very important and 5 is extremely important. You don't need to fill out all the spaces.

PROS	1-5	CONS	1-5
TOTAL		TOTAL	

Add up the totals. What is your conclusion and what are your next steps?

_____

_____

Date:

Write down the decision you want to analyze.

_____

_____

Write down the pros (positives) and cons (negatives) related to the above. Give each one a number, 1-5 where 1 is not very important and 5 is extremely important. You don't need to fill out all the spaces.

PROS	1-5	CONS	1-5
TOTAL		TOTAL	

Add up the totals. What is your conclusion and what are your next steps?

_____

_____

Date:

Write down the decision you want to analyze.

_____

_____

Write down the pros (positives) and cons (negatives) related to the above. Give
each one a number, 1-5 where 1 is not very important and 5 is extremely
important. You don't need to fill out all the spaces.

PROS	1-5	CONS	1-5
TOTAL		TOTAL	

Add up the totals. What is your conclusion and what are your next steps?

_____

_____

Date:

Write down the decision you want to analyze.

_____

_____

Write down the pros (positives) and cons (negatives) related to the above. Give each one a number, 1-5 where 1 is not very important and 5 is extremely important. You don't need to fill out all the spaces.

PROS	1-5	CONS	1-5
TOTAL		TOTAL	

Add up the totals. What is your conclusion and what are your next steps?

_____

_____

Date:

Write down the decision you want to analyze.

_____

_____

Write down the pros (positives) and cons (negatives) related to the above. Give each one a number, 1-5 where 1 is not very important and 5 is extremely important. You don't need to fill out all the spaces.

PROS	1-5	CONS	1-5
TOTAL		TOTAL	

Add up the totals. What is your conclusion and what are your next steps?

_____

_____

Date:

Write down the decision you want to analyze.

_____

_____

Write down the pros (positives) and cons (negatives) related to the above. Give each one a number, 1-5 where 1 is not very important and 5 is extremely important. You don't need to fill out all the spaces.

PROS	1-5	CONS	1-5
TOTAL		TOTAL	

Add up the totals. What is your conclusion and what are your next steps?

_____

_____

Date:

Write down the decision you want to analyze.

_____

_____

Write down the pros (positives) and cons (negatives) related to the above. Give each one a number, 1-5 where 1 is not very important and 5 is extremely important. You don't need to fill out all the spaces.

PROS	1-5	CONS	1-5
TOTAL		TOTAL	

Add up the totals. What is your conclusion and what are your next steps?

_____

_____

Date:

Write down the decision you want to analyze.

_____

_____

Write down the pros (positives) and cons (negatives) related to the above. Give each one a number, 1-5 where 1 is not very important and 5 is extremely important. You don't need to fill out all the spaces.

PROS	1-5	CONS	1-5
TOTAL		TOTAL	

Add up the totals. What is your conclusion and what are your next steps?

_____

_____

Date:

Write down the decision you want to analyze.

_____

_____

Write down the pros (positives) and cons (negatives) related to the above. Give each one a number, 1-5 where 1 is not very important and 5 is extremely important. You don't need to fill out all the spaces.

PROS	1-5	CONS	1-5
TOTAL		TOTAL	

Add up the totals. What is your conclusion and what are your next steps?

_____

_____

Date:

Write down the decision you want to analyze.

_____

_____

Write down the pros (positives) and cons (negatives) related to the above. Give each one a number, 1-5 where 1 is not very important and 5 is extremely important. You don't need to fill out all the spaces.

PROS	1-5	CONS	1-5
TOTAL		TOTAL	

Add up the totals. What is your conclusion and what are your next steps?

_____

_____

Date:

Write down the decision you want to analyze.

_____

_____

Write down the pros (positives) and cons (negatives) related to the above. Give each one a number, 1-5 where 1 is not very important and 5 is extremely important. You don't need to fill out all the spaces.

PROS	1-5	CONS	1-5
TOTAL		TOTAL	

Add up the totals. What is your conclusion and what are your next steps?

_____

_____

Date:

Write down the decision you want to analyze.

_____

_____

Write down the pros (positives) and cons (negatives) related to the above. Give each one a number, 1-5 where 1 is not very important and 5 is extremely important. You don't need to fill out all the spaces.

PROS	1-5	CONS	1-5
TOTAL		TOTAL	

Add up the totals. What is your conclusion and what are your next steps?

_____

_____

Date:

Write down the decision you want to analyze.

_____

_____

Write down the pros (positives) and cons (negatives) related to the above. Give each one a number, 1-5 where 1 is not very important and 5 is extremely important. You don't need to fill out all the spaces.

PROS	1-5	CONS	1-5
TOTAL		TOTAL	

Add up the totals. What is your conclusion and what are your next steps?

_____

_____

Date:

Write down the decision you want to analyze.

_____

_____

Write down the pros (positives) and cons (negatives) related to the above. Give each one a number, 1-5 where 1 is not very important and 5 is extremely important. You don't need to fill out all the spaces.

PROS	1-5	CONS	1-5
TOTAL		TOTAL	

Add up the totals. What is your conclusion and what are your next steps?

_____

_____

Date:

Write down the decision you want to analyze.

_____

_____

Write down the pros (positives) and cons (negatives) related to the above. Give each one a number, 1-5 where 1 is not very important and 5 is extremely important. You don't need to fill out all the spaces.

PROS	1-5	CONS	1-5
TOTAL		TOTAL	

Add up the totals. What is your conclusion and what are your next steps?

_____

_____

Date:

Write down the decision you want to analyze.

_____

_____

Write down the pros (positives) and cons (negatives) related to the above. Give
each one a number, 1-5 where 1 is not very important and 5 is extremely
important. You don't need to fill out all the spaces.

PROS	1-5	CONS	1-5
TOTAL		TOTAL	

Add up the totals. What is your conclusion and what are your next steps?

_____

_____

Date:

Write down the decision you want to analyze.

_____

_____

Write down the pros (positives) and cons (negatives) related to the above. Give each one a number, 1-5 where 1 is not very important and 5 is extremely important. You don't need to fill out all the spaces.

PROS	1-5	CONS	1-5
TOTAL		TOTAL	

Add up the totals. What is your conclusion and what are your next steps?

_____

_____

Date:

Write down the decision you want to analyze.

_____

_____

Write down the pros (positives) and cons (negatives) related to the above. Give each one a number, 1-5 where 1 is not very important and 5 is extremely important. You don't need to fill out all the spaces.

PROS	1-5	CONS	1-5
TOTAL		TOTAL	

Add up the totals. What is your conclusion and what are your next steps?

_____

_____

Date:

Write down the decision you want to analyze.

_____

_____

Write down the pros (positives) and cons (negatives) related to the above. Give each one a number, 1-5 where 1 is not very important and 5 is extremely important. You don't need to fill out all the spaces.

PROS	1-5	CONS	1-5
TOTAL		TOTAL	

Add up the totals. What is your conclusion and what are your next steps?

_____

_____

Date:

Write down the decision you want to analyze.

_____

_____

Write down the pros (positives) and cons (negatives) related to the above. Give each one a number, 1-5 where 1 is not very important and 5 is extremely important. You don't need to fill out all the spaces.

PROS	1-5	CONS	1-5
TOTAL		TOTAL	

Add up the totals. What is your conclusion and what are your next steps?

_____

_____

Date:

Write down the decision you want to analyze.

_____

_____

Write down the pros (positives) and cons (negatives) related to the above. Give each one a number, 1-5 where 1 is not very important and 5 is extremely important. You don't need to fill out all the spaces.

PROS	1-5	CONS	1-5
TOTAL		TOTAL	

Add up the totals. What is your conclusion and what are your next steps?

_____

_____

Date:

Write down the decision you want to analyze.

_____

_____

Write down the pros (positives) and cons (negatives) related to the above. Give each one a number, 1-5 where 1 is not very important and 5 is extremely important. You don't need to fill out all the spaces.

PROS	1-5	CONS	1-5
TOTAL		TOTAL	

Add up the totals. What is your conclusion and what are your next steps?

_____

_____

Date:

Write down the decision you want to analyze.

_____

_____

Write down the pros (positives) and cons (negatives) related to the above. Give each one a number, 1-5 where 1 is not very important and 5 is extremely important. You don't need to fill out all the spaces.

PROS	1-5	CONS	1-5
TOTAL		TOTAL	

Add up the totals. What is your conclusion and what are your next steps?

_____

_____

Date:

Write down the decision you want to analyze.

_____

_____

Write down the pros (positives) and cons (negatives) related to the above. Give each one a number, 1-5 where 1 is not very important and 5 is extremely important. You don't need to fill out all the spaces.

PROS	1-5	CONS	1-5
TOTAL		TOTAL	

Add up the totals. What is your conclusion and what are your next steps?

_____

_____

Date:

Write down the decision you want to analyze.

_____

_____

Write down the pros (positives) and cons (negatives) related to the above. Give each one a number, 1-5 where 1 is not very important and 5 is extremely important. You don't need to fill out all the spaces.

PROS	1-5	CONS	1-5
TOTAL		TOTAL	

Add up the totals. What is your conclusion and what are your next steps?

_____

_____

Date:

PROS	1-5	CONS	1-5
TOTAL		TOTAL	

Add up the totals. What is your conclusion and what are your next steps?

_____

_____

Date:

PROS	1-5	CONS	1-5
TOTAL		TOTAL	

Add up the totals. What is your conclusion and what are your next steps?

_____

_____

Date:

PROS	1-5	CONS	1-5
TOTAL		TOTAL	

Add up the totals. What is your conclusion and what are your next steps?

_____

_____

Date:

PROS	1-5	CONS	1-5
TOTAL		TOTAL	

Add up the totals. What is your conclusion and what are your next steps?

_____

_____

Date:

PROS	1-5	CONS	1-5
TOTAL		TOTAL	

Add up the totals. What is your conclusion and what are your next steps?

_____

_____

Date:

PROS	1-5	CONS	1-5
TOTAL		TOTAL	

Add up the totals. What is your conclusion and what are your next steps?

_____

_____

Date:

PROS	1-5	CONS	1-5
TOTAL		TOTAL	

Add up the totals. What is your conclusion and what are your next steps?

_____

_____

Date:

PROS	1-5	CONS	1-5
TOTAL		TOTAL	

Add up the totals. What is your conclusion and what are your next steps?

Date:

PROS	1-5	CONS	1-5
TOTAL		TOTAL	

Add up the totals. What is your conclusion and what are your next steps?

_____

_____

Date:

PROS	1-5	CONS	1-5
TOTAL		TOTAL	

Add up the totals. What is your conclusion and what are your next steps?

_____

_____

Date:

PROS	1-5	CONS	1-5
TOTAL		TOTAL	

Add up the totals. What is your conclusion and what are your next steps?

www.ingramcontent.com/pod-product-compliance
Lightning Source LLC
Chambersburg PA
CBHW030946240526
45463CB00016B/1969